W9-BJU-370

Watching Desert Wildlife

Watching
Desert Wildlife

by Caroline Arnold   photographs by Arthur Arnold

A Carolrhoda Nature Watch Book

Carolrhoda Books, Inc./Minneapolis

We want to thank Les and Kay Scheaffer, whose
love of the desert helped inspire this project, and
Stephen Scheaffer, Matthew Arnold, Jennifer Arnold,
Humberto Gutierrez, and Peter Waser for their
assistance with the photographs. We also thank
Sandy Cudmore for sharing her desert tortoises
with us. We are also grateful for the resources of
Anza-Borrego State Park, the Living Desert Reserve,
and the Los Angeles Zoo in California and the
Sonora Desert Museum in Arizona.

Additional photographs courtesy of: Caroline Arnold, pp. 7,
12 (left), 27 (top left), 29 (right), 48 (right); Stephen Scheaffer,
p. 31; Lynn M. Stone, pp. 34 (top), 38; R. E. Barber, pp. 37, 41
(bottom); Jerry Hennen, p. 39 (top); Peter Waser, p. 40 (top);
Matthew Arnold, p. 43 (top); Richard Hewett, p. 48 (left).

Text copyright © 1994 by Caroline Arnold
Photographs copyright © 1994 by Arthur Arnold

Carolrhoda Books, Inc. c/o The Lerner Group
241 First Avenue North, Minneapolis, MN 55401

LIBRARY OF CONGRESS CATALOGING-IN-PUBLICATION DATA

T 52059

Arnold, Caroline.
    Watching desert wildlife / by Caroline Arnold ; photographs
by Arthur Arnold.
        p.   cm.
    "A Carolrhoda nature watch book"
    Includes index.
    ISBN 0-87614-841-0 (lib. bdg.)
    1. Desert biology—Juvenile literature. 2. Deserts—Juvenile
literature. [1. Desert biology. 2. Deserts.] I. Arnold, Arthur, ill.
II. Title.
QH88.a76 1994
574.5'2652—dc20
                                        93-48076
                                          CIP
                                           AC

Manufactured in the United States of America

1 2 3 4 5 6 – I/JR – 99 98 97 96 95 94

TABLE OF CONTENTS

Introduction   7
What Is a Desert?   9
Deserts of the World   10
Deserts of North America   13
Finding Water in the Desert   14
Coping with Extreme
Temperatures   18
The Living Desert   22
Plants   22
Birds   32
Reptiles   36
Mammals   40
Glossary   46
Index   47
About the Author and
Photographer   48

The blooms of the barrel cactus attract many desert insects.

While roadrunners chase after snakes, lizards, and other small animals, they can maintain speeds of more than 15 miles per hour (24 kilometers per hour).

INTRODUCTION

The scent of a blooming barrel cactus fills the desert air as a roadrunner scans the landscape for its morning meal. When a moving shadow reveals a lizard, the roadrunner dashes over with lightning speed and snatches the lizard in its bill.

Most of us think of the desert as a barren, lifeless place. Yet, if you look closely, you will find a wide variety of plants and animals. Each of them has adapted to the harsh climate and has made the desert its home. From the tiny kangaroo rat to the speedy roadrunner to the prickly cactus, every form of life in the desert has developed ways to cope with lack of water, extreme temperatures, and the difficulty of finding food and shelter.

Lizards warm up in the morning sun.

The deserts of the southwestern United States are perfect places for observing the amazing ways in which plants and animals interact with one another and with their desert surroundings. A community of plants and animals that live in the same environment is called an **ecosystem.** Plants and animals that live in desert ecosystems share the challenge of trying to survive in some of the driest places on earth.

7

Cacti are common in many of the North American deserts. These desert plants can survive in places where there is little water.

WHAT IS A DESERT?

Deserts cover about one-seventh of the earth's land surface and are found on every continent except Europe and Antarctica. Desert landscapes vary greatly, but all deserts have one thing in common: they are extremely dry. There is little rain or snow, and whatever moisture does fall usually evaporates, or dries, quickly. Most scientists agree that a desert is a place with less than 10 inches (25 centimeters) of rain in a year. By comparison, most nondesert areas in the central and eastern United States receive more than 40 inches (1 meter) of rain in a year. In the Atacama Desert in Chile, no rain has fallen during the last 40 years! The Atacama is the driest place on earth. For plants and animals that live in the desert, the challenge is to make the most of the little water that is available.

Although we tend to think of deserts as hot, sandy places, they are made of more than just sand. The largest desert in the world is the Sahara in Africa. There, more than 3 million square miles (7.8 million square kilometers) of rocks, mountains, and hot, shifting sands stretch from the Red Sea to the Atlantic Ocean. Only about one-fifth of the world's deserts are sandy, and not all of them are hot. The landscape of most deserts, including many portions of those in the United States, is rocky or mountainous.

Some scientists consider polar regions to be deserts because these areas receive little moisture. However, because of the extreme cold, plants and animals that live near the poles are much different from those that live in the hot deserts of the world.

Deserts of the World

Most deserts, including the Sahara, Kalahari, Arabian, Indian, and Australian Deserts, are located near the Tropics. The tropic of Cancer is an imaginary line around the earth about 1,600 miles (2,560 km) north of the equator. The tropic of Capricorn is a line the same distance south of the equator. In the area between the Tropics, the earth is closest to the sun. There, the sun is almost directly overhead at noon during much of the year, and the weather is generally hot.

Deserts form in the Tropics because of wind patterns along the equator. Sunlight at the equator causes warm air to rise. As the air rises, it cools, and the moisture in it falls as rain. The air flows north and south from the equator, and when it returns to the earth along the Tropics, it is so dry that clouds cannot form. Without clouds and the rains that clouds bring, these regions become deserts.

Some deserts, such as the Great Basin Desert in the western United States, form because tall mountains act as barriers to prevent rain clouds from reaching them. The clouds drop their moisture before rising over the mountains. These inland deserts lie in areas called **rain shadows.**

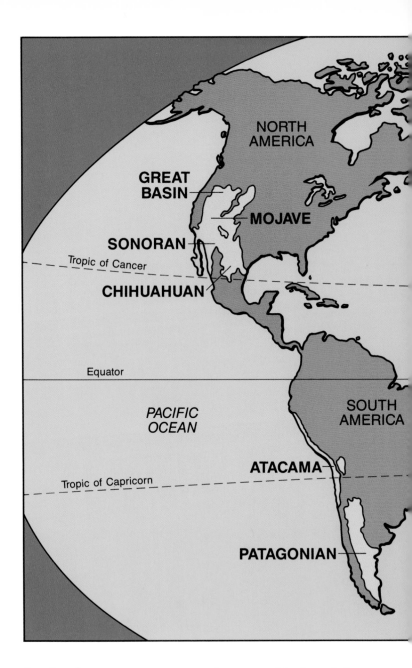

Such deserts are sometimes called cold deserts because they are hot in summer but cold in winter.

The Namib Desert in Africa and the Atacama Desert in Chile are the result of cold-water currents in the Atlantic

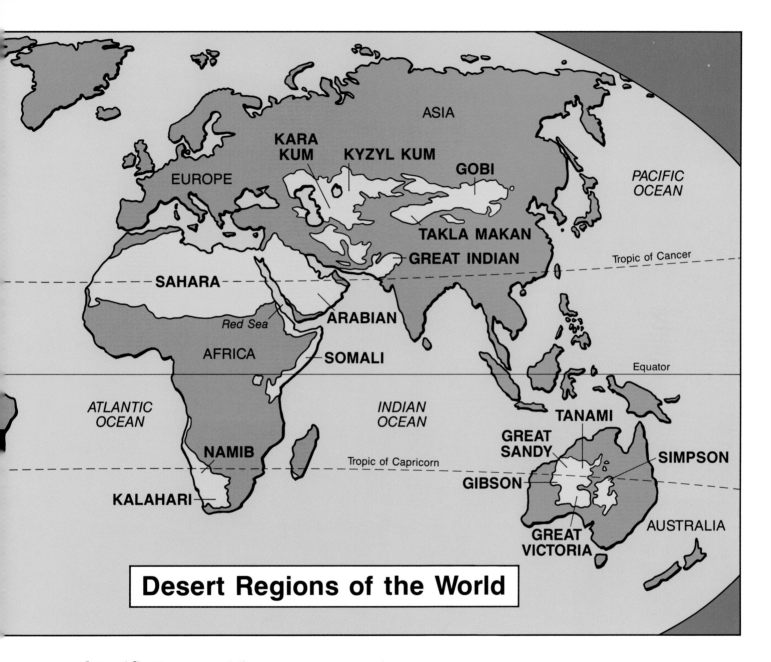

Desert Regions of the World

and Pacific Oceans. These currents cool the air that passes over them. When air is cooled, it drops its moisture as rain. By the time the air reaches land, it is so dry that the land it flows over becomes a desert.

11

Unusual rock formations, such as these in Monument Valley in northern Arizona, are typical of the Great Basin Desert.

This saguaro cactus in the Sonoran Desert is more than 100 years old.

Deserts of North America

North America's four major deserts are found in the western and southwestern United States and in Mexico. They are the Great Basin, Sonoran, Mojave [muh-HAHV-ee], and Chihuahuan [chee-WA-wan] Deserts.

The Great Basin Desert is a large, dry **plateau,** or flat highland, located between the Rocky Mountains and the Sierra Nevada. It extends into Utah, Nevada, Wyoming, Idaho, Oregon, and northern Arizona. Because much of this land is at high elevations, it is not as hot as deserts farther to the south.

The Sonoran Desert covers parts of Arizona, California, and the Mexican state of Sonora, on either side of the Sea of Cortés. At the Sonoran Desert's eastern edge, you can see thousands of giant saguaro [suh-WAHR-oh] cacti dotting the hilly landscape.

The landscape of the Mojave Desert in California and southern Nevada is similar in many ways to the Sonoran Desert. The Mojave is slightly higher and wetter.

Joshua trees are large members of the lily family. They are unique to the Mojave Desert.

The Chihuahuan Desert extends from the Mexican state of Chihuahua north into Texas and New Mexico. This desert is extremely hot and dry.

Each of the North American deserts has its own unique features, but all four deserts share many characteristics and have **species,** or kinds, of wildlife in common. The plants and animals that live in these deserts face many of the same problems in their struggle to survive.

13

Water brought by winter storms rushes along a creek bed.

Finding Water in the Desert

In most deserts, moisture falls in just a few months of each year. During the rest of the year, there is little or no rain at all. In the Great Basin Desert, most water comes from winter snow, while in the Sonoran Desert in Arizona, most water comes from summer thunderstorms. The rainy season in the California deserts is in the winter.

In a storm, rain pours down hillsides, quickly filling gullies and riverbeds. Dry streambeds, sometimes called **arroyos** [uh-ROY-ohz], can fill with rushing torrents during flash floods. As the water tumbles forward, it pushes ahead rocks, sticks, plants, and whatever else is in its way. Then, when the rain stops, the water sinks into the earth, and the stream becomes dry once again.

Cracked mud plates are all that remain after a flash flood. They provide hiding places for crickets and other desert insects.

Bladderpod is a common shrub along desert arroyos.

Flash floods can come without warning and are dangerous. It is not a good idea to walk along the bottom of a streambed during the rainy season.

Some desert plants depend on flash floods to get started growing. Their seeds have tough outer coats. As seeds bounce against rock or gravel in a flash flood, their protective coats wear off. Then the seeds can sprout, and the water that has soaked into the ground helps them grow.

For a short time after a heavy rain, pools of water may remain in the desert. They become home to frogs and toads, which need a damp environment to lay their eggs. When the eggs hatch, the tadpoles grow quickly into adults. Then, when the rainy season ends, the hot sun bakes the earth dry. Frogs and toads survive during dry periods by going underground. They may stay there for a year or more, resting and waiting until heavy rains come again.

The fan palm's datelike fruit is eaten by many desert animals.

At an oasis, you might see a fish-eating bird such as this night heron.

Some of the rainwater that soaks into the earth collects in underground rivers and lakes. Sometimes this water flows to the surface to make small ponds or water holes. In the desert, these permanent supplies of water are called **oases.** There, water-loving plants can grow and animals gather to drink, cool off, and, in some cases, make their homes.

Oases are easy to spot because tall trees often grow there. Palm trees grow in warm climates, but they need a great deal of water to live. In the desert, they are a sign of an oasis. The palm tree gets moisture from water near the surface of the soil. Thousands of tiny roots spread out around the base of the tree and form a dense mat on the ground. This covering prevents other plants from intruding and helps keep the soil damp.

The Washingtonia fan palm, named after the first president of the United States, is the largest palm in North America and the only native palm in California. It grows in several California deserts. (Nonnative palm species also grow in California, but they were imported from other places.) Dry palm fronds fall down from the fan palm and form a "skirt" around the tree trunk. The fallen fronds provide places for animals and birds to live. In Hawaii, these palms are called hula trees, because they look like the grass skirts worn by hula dancers.

Coping with Extreme Temperatures

The lack of clouds and nearness to the equator make most deserts hot. The world-record temperature of 136° Fahrenheit (58° Celsius) was set in the Libyan Desert, part of the Sahara in North Africa. The hottest temperature in North America was recorded at Death Valley, California, in the Mojave Desert in 1913. It was 134°F (57°C)!

In summer at midday, air temperatures in the deserts of the southwestern United States may be 110°F (43°C) or more. Because the ground absorbs the sun's heat, the earth's surface may be as hot as 160°F (71°C). Most animals cannot survive if their body temperatures rise to much more than 100°F (38°C).

Desert temperatures can change greatly from day to night. Dry desert air heats up quickly when warmed by the sun during the day. It also cools off quickly, so when night falls, the temperature drops rapidly. Even in the hottest deserts, nighttime temperatures can be close to freezing. Animals that live in the desert year-round must be able to keep warm and cool.

Many animals escape the desert's heat by going underground during the day. When the outside air is scorching, the temperature 18 inches (46 cm) below the surface of the earth may be as much as 40°F (22°C) cooler. Underground burrows are also more humid than the outside air, because they trap the tiny drops of water that an animal gives off when it breathes out.

The scorpion's hard outer shell helps it keep moisture inside its body. Scorpions often bury themselves in the sand to avoid the hot sun.

A prairie dog stands at the entrance to its burrow and watches for animals such as coyotes and eagles. At the first sign of danger, the prairie dog dives into its hole.

The burrowing owl is only 10 inches (25 cm) tall. When threatened, it puffs out its feathers to make itself look bigger than its true size.

Prairie dogs, which live in several North American deserts, build extensive underground burrows. At high elevations in the desert, prairie dogs use their burrows to escape both summer heat and winter cold. In freezing winter weather, when the ground is warmer than the outside air, the prairie dogs' burrows help them stay dry and cozy.

Vacant burrows make good homes for other desert animals. The burrowing owl, for example, makes its home in holes in the ground. During the day, the owl sits at the entrance to its nest. At dusk, it goes hunting for food.

Although some animals, such as ground squirrels, move about during the day, they rarely venture out into the hot, midday sun. Animals that feed during the day are usually most active either in the early morning or late afternoon.

Many desert animals go out at night to avoid the sun's heat. Night is the time for **nocturnal** creatures, those that move about at night and sleep during the day. Owls emerge from their holes and search on silent wings for rats and mice and other small animals. Desert bats leave caves and deep rock crevices to swoop and soar after tiny insects. Scorpions come out from under rocks and look for spiders and insects to eat. The small kit fox breathes the fresh evening air and gets ready to go hunting too.

The kit fox's large ears help it hear the tiny, high-pitched sounds of the rats and mice it hunts. Big ears also help the kit fox stay cool. Blood flowing through the ears allows extra body heat to pass into the outside air.

The 6-inch (15 cm) high elf owl is the smallest owl in the world. It nests in abandoned woodpecker holes in the saguaro cactus.

21

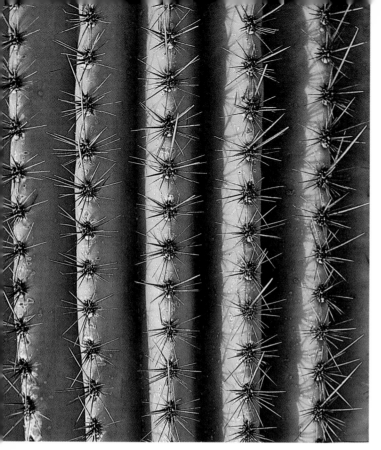

The saguaro's pleated stem allows it to expand and contract easily.

The pulpy insides of a barrel cactus are laden with water.

THE LIVING DESERT

Plants

Except at an oasis, the supply of water in the desert is scarce and unpredictable. Plants and animals in the desert have several different ways of coping with the shortage of water. One way is to store water from rainstorms for future use. Plants that can store large amounts of water in their tissues are called **succulents**.

One type of succulent, the cactus, has an amazing ability to store water and is perfectly suited to hot, desert life. Cacti are native to North and South America, but they can grow in other parts of the world where they have been introduced by people.

Cacti have shallow roots that spread out just under the surface of the ground. Even when there is little rain, the cactus can quickly absorb moisture and store it

The name of the hedgehog cactus reflects its shape.

Spines of the staghorn cactus are needle sharp.

in its thick stem. A giant saguaro cactus may take in as much as a ton (.9 metric tons) of water at one time. When filled with water, the cactus expands. Then, as the water is used, the stem shrinks.

Plants in dry climates are adapted to keep the water they do absorb from evaporating. Cacti have thick skins that help keep moisture inside. The cactus skin also has a waxy coating as further protection against water loss.

Instead of leaves, cactus plants have sharp spines. Spines help prevent desert animals from eating cacti, but they have another use as well. Although the spines are thin, they produce shadows on the cactus skin and help protect it from the hot sun. The dry, windy air of the desert removes moisture from everything it touches. Cactus spines break up hot air currents, so moisture does not evaporate as fast.

Gila woodpeckers use their strong beaks to peck holes for nests in the saguaro cactus.

A flicker perches on top of a saguaro.

The holes made by birds do not seem to harm the cactus. Saguaros produce a sticky fluid that hardens and forms a seal around the nest cavity.

When the saguaro dies, the flesh rots away and the woody supports are all that remain. These saguaro skeletons are sometimes called "ghost" saguaros.

The saguaro cactus, which can grow to be 50 feet (15 m) tall, is among the most impressive desert plants. It is the largest species of cactus in the United States and the second largest in the world. Only the cardon cactus, which grows in Baja California, Mexico, is bigger. The bigger they grow, the more water these cacti can store. A 50-foot saguaro filled with water may weigh up to 10 tons (9 t)!

Saguaros are found only in the Sonoran Desert, and most are located in Saguaro National Monument near Tucson, Arizona. The saguaro is extremely slow growing, gaining only a few inches each year. The saguaro begins as a single spike and does not develop its first "arms" until it is 30 years old or more. Some saguaros may live to be more than 200 years old. Saguaros are endangered, or threatened with **extinction,** because they do not grow fast enough to replace those that die naturally or are destroyed or removed from the desert by people. A species becomes extinct when all of its kind die. If saguaros become extinct, animals that depend on them will lose an important resource.

Saguaros support a wide variety of desert life. Birds use their tall branches for perching and for places to build nests. In the spring, insects, birds, and bats feed on the nectar of the cactus flowers. Later, the flowers form fruits that are eaten by many desert animals and by people. When the cactus dies, insects make their homes in the rotting flesh.

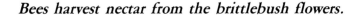
Bees harvest nectar from the brittlebush flowers.

The agave [uh-GAHV-ee], or century plant, may go for years without producing a flower. But when conditions are right, it can send up a 14-foot (4.2-m) flower stalk in just a few weeks.

Although we think of the cactus as the typical desert plant, many other kinds of plants have adapted to the desert environment. Some of them cope with long dry periods by shedding their leaves and going into a state of rest. (Plants and animals that become inactive in the summer are said to **estivate**. Those that are inactive in winter are said to **hibernate**.)

The brittlebush is a common desert bush that estivates. During late winter and spring, it produces brilliant yellow flowers. When summer comes, the flowers dry up, the leaves drop off, and the plant takes on a gray, dead appearance. Although it looks lifeless, it will turn green again as soon as the winter rains begin.

When plants grow close together, they must compete with each other for water and nutrients in the soil. The brittlebush discourages other plants from growing too close to it by releasing a poisonous chemical into the surrounding soil. With little or no competition, the brittlebush gets all the moisture and nutrients for itself.

An ocotillo plant may grow 10 to 20 feet (3 to 6 m) tall.

New leaves emerge from the spiny branch of an ocotillo.

The ocotillo [oh-coh-TEE-yoh] is another common desert plant. In summer, its stalks look bare and dead. But within a few days after a rain has soaked the earth, tiny leaves appear. Later, brilliant orange flowers bloom at the tops of the long branches. A sticky resin along the ocotillo's branches helps keep moisture from evaporating. In the 1500s, Aztec people in Mexico called the ocotillo "candlewood" because, when the branches were burned, the resin gave them a bright flame.

27

Some plants are able to survive in the desert because they have extremely long roots that reach far into the ground to permanent sources of water. The mesquite [meh-SKEET] tree's root, for example, may grow 100 feet (30 m) deep. Because the tree has a constant supply of water, its leaves are green year-round. Mesquite is one of the most widespread desert shrubs. The thick trunk and stems of this sturdy plant are a source of firewood for many people who live in the desert.

Mesquite belongs to the same plant family as peas and beans. In the fall, it produces long, beanlike pods filled with seeds. A hard outer covering on each seed prevents water from penetrating. Without moisture, the seed cannot sprout. When mesquite seeds are eaten by desert animals, however, the covering is worn off by the animals' stomach juices. Partially digested seeds that pass through animals are ready to grow.

Small leaves help many desert plants conserve water. When leaves have a

Mesquite seeds grow in long, dark pods.

Native Americans who once lived in the deserts of California used grinding stones like these to crush seeds into flour.

28

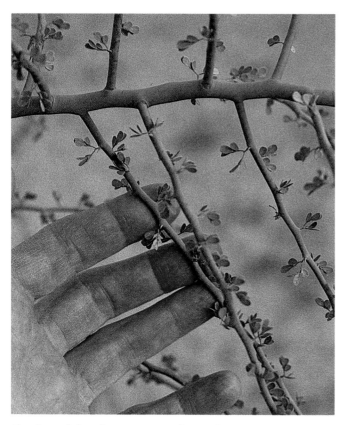

In Spanish, the name paloverde *means "green trunk."*

Smoke tree

smaller surface area, less moisture is lost to the air. The paloverde [pah-loh-VAIR-day] tree has leaves so tiny that a dozen placed side by side span only 1/2 inch (1 1/4 cm). Most plants make their own food from sunlight and **chlorophyll** [KLOR-uh-fil] in their leaves. Chlorophyll is the substance in plants that makes them green. The paloverde tree sheds its leaves in extremely hot weather, but the tree can still make its own food because it has chlorophyll in its trunk and stems.

Plants need sunlight for growth, but just like animals, they cannot live when temperatures are too high. Some desert plants, such as the smoke tree, have light-colored or shiny leaves. These help reflect the sun's hot rays. The smoke tree gets its name because of its light gray bark and leaves. It is often seen along desert streambeds.

Another way that plants survive in the desert is by limiting their lives to times when conditions are favorable for growth. Many desert flowers are **annuals,** or plants that go through their entire life cycle during a period of a few weeks or months in a single year. Most desert annuals live for just a few weeks each spring. Their seeds sprout and grow quickly into mature plants. Then they produce flowers, develop seeds, wither, and die. The wind scatters their seeds across the ground, where they lie until the next season's rain starts the cycle again.

Weather conditions must be just right to promote the growth of spring flowers. Enough rain must fall to provide moisture for the plant's whole life span. In dry years, flower seeds may remain **dormant.** They are alive but inactive, waiting for the right combination of warmth and rain. In years when water soaks the earth, the seeds sprout and the desert erupts in a carpet of color.

Sand verbena

Dune primroses and sunflowers

Desert lily

Bigelow mimulus

31

The phainopepla feeds on hackberries, the fruit of a common desert shrub.

The Gambel's quail has a distinctive plume on its head.

Birds

The bird population in the desert also varies with the time of year. Some birds, such as the cactus wren, live in the desert year-round. They are able to withstand the heat and to find food. Other birds are seasonal visitors, staying in spring and fall, but leaving when the weather becomes too hot or too cold. The phainopepla [fay-noh-PEP-luh], for instance, nests in the desert in spring and then migrates to cooler places in summer.

Each species of bird has adapted to finding food in the desert. The Gambel's quail, a ground-dwelling bird, uses its sharp claws to scratch the ground for seeds. It can survive with little water in its diet. Cactus wrens, hawks, and roadrunners get most of the moisture they need from the insects, lizards, and other small animals they eat. Other birds, such as thrushes and doves, depend on water holes for drinking. Some birds will fly many miles between their nesting grounds and a source of water.

Several species of hummingbirds thrive in the desert. Nectar in the long, tubular flowers of the chuparosa [choo-puh-RO-suh] bush is one of the hummingbird's favorite sources of food and moisture. (*Chuparosa* is the Spanish word for hummingbird.) As the hummingbird feeds, it spreads pollen from flower to flower and helps the chuparosa grow. The chuparosa blooms throughout the cooler months of the year.

Anna's hummingbird

The long bill of the hummingbird perfectly fits chuparosa flowers.

Cactus wren

Western oriole

A nest high in a paloverde tree is safe from predators.

Because there are few trees in the desert, birds often have a difficult time finding a suitable place to build a nest. A good nest site should offer some protection from the weather and be close to sources of food and water. It should also be safe from **predators**, animals that hunt and kill other animals for food. Cactus wrens and roadrunners build their nests among the thorny branches of the cholla [CHOY-uh] cactus. The thick branches provide some shade, and the sharp spines keep away most predators. Western orioles attach their nests to the stiff leaves of the yucca plant. Burrowing owls raise their babies underground. The prairie falcon and red-tailed hawk prefer to nest on high cliff ledges.

This cactus provides a safe nest site for a roadrunner.

Reptiles

Reptiles that live in the desert include snakes, lizards, and tortoises. A reptile's body temperature changes with the temperature of the surrounding air. (**Mammals** and birds, in contrast, are able to maintain a more or less constant body temperature.) At cooler temperatures, a reptile's body processes slow down. A snake or lizard needs to warm up so it can move about and hunt for food.

Just like other animals, however, snakes, lizards, and tortoises can die from too much heat. Most reptiles cannot stand to be more than 105°F (41°C). The desert iguana is unique among reptiles in that it can survive temperatures up to 117°F (47°C).

Gopher snakes are common nonvenomous snakes of the desert.

The brown and gray coloring of the western diamondback rattlesnake helps it hide among the rocks and shadows of the desert. The snake shakes the rattles in its tail as a warning to intruders.

Most desert snakes are active only on warm summer nights. By day, they hide from the heat under rocks or in holes in the ground. In winter, when the weather is cool, they hibernate underground.

Most snakes are predators and hunt insects and other small animals for their food. The animals that they hunt are their **prey**. A rattlesnake uses long fangs in the front of its mouth to inject venom, or poison, into the rabbits, lizards, and other small animals that are its prey. It will not attack large animals or people, except in defense. The bite of a rattlesnake is painful and dangerous, so when you are walking or climbing in places where rattlesnakes live, be sure to look before you step or before placing your hand on a ledge.

The Gila [HEE-luh] monster is the only venomous lizard that lives in the United States. Although its bite is painful to humans, it is almost never fatal. The Gila monster can go for long periods without food by living on the fat stored in its thick tail. When it is hungry, it looks for eggs and small animals. It grasps its prey in its jaws and bites down into the flesh. Venom flows into the wound through grooves in the Gila monster's teeth.

Lizards are usually more active during the day than at night. In the early morning, you might see a lizard sunning itself on a rock. It will stay there only as long as it takes for its body to heat up. Then it will dart into the shade. Some snakes and lizards bury themselves in loose sand to get out of the sun.

The bright coloring of the Gila monster is a warning to predators.

A lizard pauses briefly on a rock.

Desert tortoises get some protection from the sun from their tough outer shells. In winter, tortoises hibernate in deep holes in the ground. In spring, they emerge to mate. After the female lays her eggs in the sand, the sun keeps them warm. Three months later, the eggs hatch and the tiny tortoises are on their own. Few survive to adulthood. Many are eaten by ravens and other predators. Those that survive face other dangers. Desert tortoises are endangered because their **habitat**, or the place where they live, is being destroyed as people develop the desert for their own use.

The desert tortoise eats flowers and grass with its sharp, beaklike mouth. It gets all the moisture it needs from its food.

Mammals

More than 70 species of mammals live in the deserts of North America. Of these, at least two-thirds are **rodents,** plant-eating animals that gnaw with their teeth. Among the most common desert rodents are pocket mice, deer mice, pack rats, and kangaroo rats.

The tiny kangaroo rat has long hind legs on which it hops like a kangaroo. When the kangaroo rat finds seeds, it stuffs them into large pouches in its cheeks. When it returns to its burrow, it empties the pouches and stores the seeds to eat later. The kangaroo rat finds most of the moisture it needs in its food, so it hardly ever drinks. If the kangaroo rat is extremely thirsty, it may gnaw on a barrel cactus to get at the watery pulp. The kangaroo rat can also manufacture water in its own body.

In the pack rat's cool, moist burrow, you might find a collection of seeds, leaves, flowers, twigs, bones, and other small objects. Pack rats store all kinds of things in their burrows. They may use the same burrow for many years, and when they clean out, they throw their trash in a pile near the burrow entrance. The pack rat's garbage heap provides clues to scientists about changing conditions in the desert.

A kangaroo rat can leap several feet in one hop. This helps it avoid predators.

Pack rats often build burrows under clumps of prickly pear cactus. The thorny cactus helps protect them from other animals, and the pack rats eat the prickly pear fruit.

40

A mother peccary nuzzles her youngster.

The light coloring of the cottontail rabbit makes it hard to see against the rocky or sandy ground.

Jackrabbits and cottontail rabbits are some other plant eaters in the desert. They prefer to nibble on leafy green plants but sometimes eat cactus when they need water. Sharp front teeth help them penetrate the cactus's tough skin.

Wild pigs called peccaries [PEK-uh-reez] also eat cacti. Peccaries live in the Sonoran Desert in Arizona, in parts of New Mexico and Texas, and in Central and South America. They are sometimes called javelinas. These night feeders dig up roots of cacti and other plants for food, but they will also eat fruit, snakes, or lizards. Peccaries usually forage in groups.

The coyote is one of the most often seen large mammals of the desert. Along with the kit fox, it is a member of the dog family. The coyote is able to live in a wide variety of habitats because it is extremely adaptable. It will eat whatever it can find—insects, lizards, snakes, birds, rodents, rabbits, fruit, nuts, grass, and young tortoises. Where people live in the desert, coyotes sometimes raid garbage cans for food too. Coyotes need to drink water regularly and sometimes dig holes in dry creek beds to find water that lies just under the surface.

Mountain lions, also called pumas or cougars, roam the high desert. They feed on deer, mountain sheep, peccaries, and other large animals. They are active mostly at night. Like other cats, they can see well in the dark, and this helps them stalk their prey. When they get close enough to attack, they pounce and kill the animal with their sharp teeth and claws.

Bighorn sheep are also found at higher elevations in the deserts of the southwestern United States. These large, sure-footed animals climb nimbly on steep rocky slopes. They eat grasses and plants that grow between the rocks. Thick wool helps protect the sheep from the sun during the day and keeps them warm at night. Desert bighorn have adapted well to their environment, but they are threatened with extinction both from hunting and from loss of their natural habitat.

Hunters in the Mojave Desert made these drawings of bighorn sheep more than 2,000 years ago.

Mountain lions need to drink regularly, so they do not go far from a source of water.

43

In many parts of the world, people live in or near deserts. Irrigation systems that bring water to the desert make it possible to grow crops and build cities. With reliable sources of water, people have made the desert bloom.

Every year thousands more people visit the desert to enjoy the scenery and to learn about the diversity of desert wildlife. Yet, as people push cities, farms, and recreation areas farther into desert regions, plants and animals that live in these areas become threatened.

The desert is a beautiful and amazing place, populated by plants and animals that have adapted in unique ways to extreme temperatures, little water, and limited resources for food and shelter. Most living things could not survive in the harsh conditions of the desert, but for those that have made it their home, the desert provides everything they need to live. Only by preserving the desert environment can we help these plants and animals continue to survive. And only if we ensure their survival will we have the opportunity to learn more about the secrets of their success.

GLOSSARY

annuals: plants that complete their life cycles in one growing season

arroyos: dry streambeds

chlorophyll: the substance in plants that makes them green

dormant: being in a state in which a seed or plant is alive but not growing

ecosystem: a particular environment and the plants and animals that live in it

estivate: to be inactive in the summer

extinction: the state in which no members of a species are left alive

habitat: the specific kind of area where an animal or plant naturally lives

hibernate: to be inactive in the winter

mammals: animals with hair or fur that produce milk to feed their young and maintain a constant body temperature

nocturnal: being most active at night

oases: permanent supplies of water in the desert

plateau: a flat highland

predators: animals that hunt other animals for food

prey: animals that are hunted for food

rain shadows: areas that get little rainfall because tall mountains prevent rain clouds from reaching them

reptiles: scaly vertebrates, such as snakes and lizards, that creep or crawl

rodents: plant-eating mammals that gnaw with their teeth

species: a group of plants or animals that share similar characteristics and can interbreed

succulents: plants that can store large amounts of water

INDEX

arroyos, 14
Atacama Desert, 9, 10

bighorn sheep, 42
birds, 32-35, 36; cactus wren, 32, 35; desert bat, 21; doves, 32; Gambel's quail, 32; hawks, 32, 35; hummingbirds, 33; owls, 19, 21, 35; phainopepla, 32; prairie falcon, 35; roadrunner, 7, 32, 35; thrushes, 32; Western oriole, 35
burrowing animals, 18-19, 40

cacti, 22-25, 41; barrel cactus, 7; cardon cactus, 25; cholla cactus, 35. *See also* saguaro cactus
California deserts, 13, 14, 17, 18
Chihuahuan Desert, 13
chlorophyll, 29
coyote, 42

Death Valley, CA, 18
deer mice, 40
deserts, definition of, 9; extremes of temperature in, 7, 18-21, 44; formation of, 10-11; impact of people on, 25, 39, 44; scarcity of food and shelter in, 7, 35, 44; scarcity of water in, 7, 9, 14-17, 22, 44; where located, 7, 9, 10
dormancy, 30

ecosystem, 7
estivation, 26

flash floods, 14, 15
frogs, 15

Great Basin Desert, 10, 13, 14
ground squirrels, 21

hibernation, 26, 37

kangaroo rats, 7, 40
kit fox, 21, 42

mammals, 36, 40-42
Mojave Desert, 13, 18
mountain lion, 42

Native Americans, 27, 28
nocturnal animals, 21

oases, 17

pack rats, 40
peccaries, 41
plants, 15, 22-30; brittlebush, 26; chuparosa bush, 33; flowers, 30; mesquite tree, 28; ocotillo, 27; palm trees, 17; paloverde tree, 29; smoke tree, 29; succulents, 22; yucca plant, 35. *See also* cacti
pocket mice, 40
prairie dogs, 19

rabbits, 41
rain shadows, 10
reptiles, 36-39; desert iguana, 36; Gila monster, 38; lizards, 7, 36, 38; snakes, 36, 37; tortoises, 36, 39
rodents, 40

saguaro cactus, 13, 23, 25
Saguaro National Monument, AZ, 25
Sahara Desert, 9, 10, 18
scorpions, 21
Sonoran Desert, 13, 14, 25, 41

toads, 15
Tropics, the, 10

ABOUT THE AUTHOR AND PHOTOGRAPHER

Caroline Arnold is the author of more than 90 books for young readers including the Carolrhoda Nature Watch titles *Saving the Peregrine Falcon, A Walk on the Great Barrier Reef, Tule Elk, Ostriches and Other Flightless Birds,* and *House Sparrows Everywhere.* She is also the author of *Cats: In from the Wild* for the Carolrhoda Understanding Animals Series. Ms. Arnold teaches part-time in the UCLA Extension Writers' Program. Her husband and collaborator, **Arthur Arnold,** is a neurobiologist at UCLA. He became interested in photography as a high school student and now takes photographs for his own scientific research and as a hobby. He was also the photographer for *A Walk on the Great Barrier Reef.* The Arnolds live in Los Angeles.